Praise for **GLORY, TOO**

"Here are poems that come from within the soul.
Nikki Grimes is not just a disciple and believer, she is
the voice of the beloved. Her work points the reader
in the direction of salvation. One will shout hallelujah
or quietly say amen when turning the pages of *Glory,
Too*. After reading the poetry of Nikki Grimes one has
a strong desire to go out into the world and spread the
good news."

—E. Ethelbert Miller, writer and literary activist,
2023 Grammy Nominee in the category of spoken word and poetry

"Nikki Grimes' poems are like a magnifying glass
held up to the Scriptures, helping us see more closely
and clearly. They are like a prism, revealing colors
previously hidden to our busy eyes. They call us to
align ourselves with a holy direction. In one poem she
invites us to 'say yes to the jewel that is Jesus,' and by
the end of the collection my heart was overflowing with
this yes."

—Christine Valters Paintner, PhD, Online Abbess of Abbey of the
Arts and author of more than 20 books on the contemplative path

T0356442

"Author C. S. Lewis insisted that a good poet doesn't say, 'look at me'; a good poet says 'look at that'—and points. This is exactly what Nikki Grimes has done in this collection. Get ready to see things in the Scriptures that you've never noticed before. Patterns and metaphors, images and insights, the tiny, tiny seed in the fertile soil of your heart. Nikki is a wayfinder, my friends. Don't miss the invitation to join her on the journey."

—Sarah Arthur, author of *Between Midnight and Dawn: A Literary Guide to Prayer for Lent, Holy Week, and Eastertide*

"Devotional, emotional and crystalline, the poems of Nikki Grimes' *Glory, Too* are thoughtful meditations on important Biblical verses. Her poetry will excite young readers still absorbing the beauty and the messages of the Bible, but it will also make longtime students of the Bible see familiar passages with a fresh eye."

—A. M. Juster, poet, author of *Wonder and Wrath*

Glory, Too

Poems

Nikki Grimes

IRON
PEN

PARACLETE PRESS
BREWSTER, MASSACHUSETTS

For Kendall Buchanan, the brother of my heart

2025 First Printing

Glory, Too: Poems

ISBN 978-1-64060-964-8

Copyright © 2025 by Nikki Grimes

The Iron Pen name and logo are trademarks of Paraclete Press.

Library of Congress Cataloging-in-Publication Data
Names: Grimes, Nikki, author.
Title: Glory, too : poems / Nikki Grimes.
Description: Brewster, Massachusetts : Iron Pen/Paraclete Press, 2024.
  Summary: "In a marriage of poetry, faith, and worship, Ms. Grimes' poems
  illuminate the Scriptures that grace every Sunday of the year. Her
  inimitable voice and imagination offer glimpses of glory we might not
  otherwise see, throughout the seasons of the year"-- Provided by
  publisher.
Identifiers: LCCN 2024036535 (print) | LCCN 2024036536 (ebook) | ISBN
  9781640609648 (trade paperback) | ISBN 9781640609655 (epub)
Subjects: LCGFT: Religious poetry.
Classification: LCC PS3557.R489982 G58 2024 (print) | LCC PS3557.R489982
  (ebook) | DDC 811/.54--dc23/eng/20240823
LC record available at https://lccn.loc.gov/2024036535
LC ebook record available at https://lccn.loc.gov/2024036536

10 9 8 7 6 5 4 3 2 1

Published by Paraclete Press
Brewster, Massachusetts
www.paracletepress.com

Printed in The United States of America

CONTENTS

FALL

WINTER

SPRING

Worship Walking

The word "worship"
trips so easily off the tongue.
I worship. You worship.
We worship together.
What could be better?
But worship is weightier,
never confined to the harmonies
of hymns wafting in the rafters
of the meeting house,
or swaying to the rhythms of the choir
when the whole congregation
is lost in the lyrics
of grace and salvation.
True worship is
sanctifying ourselves,
sacrificing our bodies,
submitting our hearts and minds
for total transformation,
by God. For God.
He's the only one able
to perform such
complex conversions.
Our part is to let him,
which is easier said than done.
Our wills always
get in the way.
So where do we begin?
By breathing this in:
Worship is living into
"I surrender all."

Romans 12:1–2

Allegiance

False gods and false prophets
run rampant in the world,
their tongues comfortably curled
around the latest lies.
Their motives may defy our logic,
but God's truth rests
with those spirits who confess
that Jesus Christ is Lord.
And what is confession?
Words without weight,
or a life lived as witness
to the Son, the Holy one, the Christ?
In today's vernacular,
confession is
the reluctant acknowledgment
of guilt, of sin,
of that for which
we are ashamed.
But we who test the spirits by the Spirit,
who rightly divide the word of truth
lived and spoken by
the Carpenter-King—
we are not ashamed, or reluctant.
We are workmen and women
prepared to give a reason
for the hope that is within us.
We declare our allegiance to the Lord
for we cannot begin
to live or love like him
otherwise.

1 John 4:1–6

Harmonious

John was confounded when the Lord
presented himself at the river Jordan
alongside those whose souls
were desperate for cleansing.
But in one sense, I suppose
it was a small thing
to be buried in the waters of baptism
when burial in a tomb was not far off,
and both would end by rising
Beloved Son,
the sinless One,
the Lord of all.
A humble act
for the King of Glory,
just one more way
to stand with humanity,
to climb into our skin
as if our sins were his own—
a servant to the end.
No wonder the Father was pleased.
Is it too much, then, that we
Gentiles of every hue and nation,
who celebrate the nonpartisan
Good News of God's great gift,
should be called to live lives
in harmony with Him,
and to sing together
Hallelujah?

Matthew 3:13–17, Acts 10:34–43

Math Mystery

Mark and the other insiders
kept a careful catalog
of the Lord's provision.
Four thousand fed here,
five thousand fed there.
Even so, they eventually
lost count
You might as well
try to tally
the grains of sand
that edge the sea
as track the Lord's
miraculous provision.
After all,
Jehovah-Jireh is
his middle name.
Yet, the minute need
rings our doorbell,
we stare down at
our empty hands,
rather than look
to the God-man
who holds the pitcher of plenty,
ready to pour it out
should any believer ask.
Blind as we can be,
I wonder when we
will finally understand
that little is much
in God's hand.

Mark 8:14–26

X-Ray Vision

"Keep your eye on the curtain,"
says the magician,
and while we do,
he cleverly disappears.
The ruse works every time
because we trust what we see.
But God reminds us,
that's not the half of it.
More than magician,
God sees into our hearts
and far into the future
he, alone, created.
Hide and seek was never
a game for the Lord,
as Philip learned.
Jesus said, "Follow me,"
and the new disciple headed out
to spread the word, keen to share it
with one Nathanael, who Jesus saw
before Philip ever found him.
"Where did you get to know me?"
asked Nathanael, mistaking Jesus
for someone with limits.
And even when he realized
Jesus was God and King,
he failed to see the future greatness
God had in mind to do.
Like me and you,
Nathanael was too focused
on the mystery of that moment.

But not to worry.
Jesus says, "Keep your eye on me.
In good time,
all will be revealed."

John 1:43–51

Rebel Rabbi

Thirsty for conversation,
Jesus goes to the well,
engages the woman there
in a lengthy chat
—a spiritual faux-pas—
a Jew talking up a Samaritan,
and a woman at that!
"I'll trade you a spring of living water
for a drink from the well," he says.
Seeing Jesus without pail or bucket,
she snickers a bit,
wondering exactly how
he plans to perform the magic trick
of lifting water from a well.
"Are you greater than
our ancestor Jacob
who gave us this well?" she asks,
her question rhetorical.
But this stranger from Galilee
has answers
she never saw coming.
He shows himself more than seer,
peering into the secrets
of her past and present,
offers her eternal life,
expounds on true worship,
reveals his divine identity.
Water and well all but forgotten,
the woman shivers
with sudden knowing:
the man before her is

the long-awaited
source of salvation.
The disciples crash the scene,
aghast to find their Rabbi
conversing with
a lowly Samaritan,
(a woman at that).
But Jesus brushes off
their unasked questions
to share a word or two with them
about true hunger and food,
about his Father's work,
about the harvest of souls
that awaits.
He leaves in his wake
a Samaritan woman
spreading the good news
of Messiah come to save us all.
When last did we have
a conversation so sacred?

John 4:5–42

Kryptonite

Superman is not without
his weaknesses.
The burning blade of Kryptonite
whittles away his strength
and for all his super-sight,
his keen eyes cannot
see through lead.
Maybe that's what
prejudice is made of.
We encounter our Samaritans,
those certain races or religions
we label as "other"
and we go blind,
unable to see heart or hurt.
But Jesus sees.
Love is all the X-ray vision
he needs to peer past
walls of difference,
to see through sin
and points of shame,
the vulnerability
of hunger or thirst
to offer us the water of life
we never knew
we were desperate for.
Then, like the woman
at the well, we are free
to dismantle our own fears
of "the other,"
take the holy cup
we've been given
and pass it on.

John 4:5–42

Where Meaning Resides

The night visitor let Jesus know
he was in on the secret.
"Rabbi, I see who you are,"
said Nicodemus. But did he?
"To see the kingdom of God,
you must be born from above"—
this mystery from a man
who routinely spoke in riddles.
Unlike his parables,
there was not even
a sliver of story here to grasp.
Retracing one's journey
from womb to world
is beyond even the realm of
Once upon a time.
Yet, Jesus was never one
to mince a word, or waste it.
Nicodemus quickly surmised
there must be meaning,
but where did it reside?
High up in the region of spirit
where the Almighty lives.
Jesus holds the key to the code.
Come closer, he coaxes.
Only then can we focus
through the telescope of his eye
to decipher divine mystery and
crack open the door of heaven.
You must be born
of water and spirit.
Yes! we say, rising
from baptismal waters.

"Of course!" we affirm,
welcoming the Holy Spirit.
But where must even
a Pharisee begin?
"Father, forgive me,
for I have sinned."

John 3:1–7

Conundrum

The darkness of night seems
somehow appropriate
for all things ethereal,
celestial, otherworldly.
A perfect time for Nicodemus
to venture into consultation
with the Rabbi
about eternal life
and the best way to breach
the kingdom of God.
The rabbi's unexpected answer
led Nicodemus to contemplate
the humanly impossible:
all six feet of him
crawling back into
his mother's womb,
the reverse journey
through the birth canal
bloodier than the first,
his poor mother
savagely ripped in half
before even this
imaginary journey
could reach its conclusion.
Baffled, Nicodemus shook
his tired head.
"How can anyone be born
after having grown old?
Can one enter a second time
into his mother's womb
and be born?"

A fair question
for a finite mind.
But the rabbi expounded
on a transformational truth
sculpted by the Infinite,
a birth fashioned
of water and spirit
wrought in the womb of God,
an upward journey
through the birth canal
from Earth to Heaven,
the loving arms of Jesus
waiting to catch the reborn,
waiting to guide each one
into this new life.
Still baffled,
Nicodemus only accepted
this miraculous mystery
when an inner voice whispered,
Don't trust your imagination.
Just believe.
Faith is where
heavenly rebirth
begins.

John 3:1–17

Paradox on Parade

The Mount of Olives,
the site of a small commission
and a necessary obedience:
Two disciples dispatched
to acquire a colt in, shall we say,
a questionable manner.
And soon thereafter, all is set
for a demonstration of
power and humility intertwined.
Here comes our King
who calls the dead to life,
who silences the roiling sea,
who gives sight to the blind
yet doesn't seem to mind
riding atop a borrowed donkey?
A living, breathing paradox,
he willingly enters the scene
of the crime to be.
"Come! Die with me,"
he invites us,
and drunk on the power
we have witnessed, we follow.
But what do we do with the love
that held our Lord to the cross
in blood and agony
he could easily have wiped away
by simply stepping down
and leaving us to pay
for our *own* sins?

How can we begin
to respond to that?
We bow our heads,
our hearts, our knees.

Luke 19:28–40, Philippians 2:5–11

Glimpse of Glory

Death comes in threes, they say
but so does life.
If I understand nothing else
of the Trinity,
that one truth sings.
The Father offers up his son,
full of power and grace;
the Son gathers the called
then sets his face
toward Jerusalem;
and the Holy Spirit makes sure
nothing is lost in translation.
There is no way to understand
the Son without the others—
except in that moment
of supreme despair
when the Son hung there
on the cross, alone,
drenched in sin, and
the Father looked away.
Yet when the Beloved died,
all hope was born for us:
A life of grace
purchased by the Son;
a place at the table of
God's heart, secured;
and a glimpse of glory through
the gift of the Holy Spirit who
guides us along each avenue
marked with suffering
till we reach home.

And so you see, the Trinity
is just that simple—
and mysterious.

John 16:12–15, Romans 5:1–5

Familiar

Our names roll off the tongue
of a loved one, just so.
The name, alone, spoken by Him
was all it took
to tear through the veil
of misery, of heartbreak
his temporary dying
left behind.
His recent warning of
his death & resurrection
was far from
every disciple's mind.
Mary could not fathom
the empty tomb, the piles
of linen wrappings
that once wound round
her beloved.
How were they just
lying there without him?
And where was *He*?
How could she whisper
her solemn, final goodbyes
without his body?
And what sense could be made
of the angels that appeared,
barely swimming into focus
through the river of tears
threatening to drown her?
Their query, "Woman,
why are you weeping?"
seemed utterly absurd.

Yet, there was something
in the Gardener's voice
that reached her,
something in his tone
that told her he had
all the answers she needed.
And then He,
who was no gardener
called her name,
as he has since called ours.
And she knew, as we know,
This was the voice
of the Beloved.

John 20:1–18

The Dawn of Despair

Jerusalem,
the setting of heartbreak.
Two disciples escape
for a needed time-out,
grief chasing them
the seven miles to Emmaus,
despair etched
in every anxious footstep.
We know the story, of course,
that the disciples feared
the redemption of Israel
was not yet to be—if at all.
We rush through this passage,
tending to be a tad haughty,
given our *superior*
historical perspective.
I, myself, am miffed
that the women's words
were not deemed enough
to settle the matter.
That aside, how often do *we*
buy the lie that all is lost,
as if the Lord's abandonment of us
was more than mere Mirage?
Never mind.
Suffice it to say Jesus showed up—
as always—meeting the disciples
on the road.
The shadow hovering
over their hearts
slowly began to lift
as the familiar stranger
joined the conversation.

Jesus, incognito,
delves into the scriptures,
spotlighting his place in
the messianic prophecies.
Finally, in the breaking of bread,
they perceive his true identity—
just in time to witness
his departure.
Thank God, his holy,
healing work in us
occurs, even when our
spiritual discernment
is on the fritz.
Lord knows,
more often than not,
like most disciples,
our witness solidifies
in hindsight.
It happens often enough
to appear to be by design,
don't you think?
Of course, we don't know
what we don't know
which is fine,
as long as we know
the Lord is always with us
on the journey.

Luke 24:13–35

Jewel

One word marks the arc
of every story.
Today, the tale begins with
Anointed,
the seed of it bulging
with a power
realized most fully
in the life and hour
of Christ.
Anointed: the Amen
we too are given,
we who receive the Son,
and are at once spirit-fueled
for the mission molded
in the shadow of the cross
and spoken at
the borrowed tomb:
Go! Preach! Teach!
Tell everyone about the Son
the chosen one
who rose from death
as promised.
God was with him
who is now with us.
Are we not now
compelled to sing
and shout the holy news
that counters the blues
of this world?
Round and round
and round it goes:

Say yes to the jewel
that is Jesus.
Receive the mercy
of redemption,
take his body and blood
and eat. Then, hit the streets
with the meat of the gospel
so the next generation
may say yes to the jewel
that is Jesus,
who resurrected as promised,
then inexplicably entrusted *us*
with the healing, saving power
of the Word—
to pass on.

Acts 10:34–43

Cocky

2000 years is a long time ago
and distance has made us cocky.
"If I were walking on water,"
we say, "*I* wouldn't have been afraid."
"*I'd* have stayed awake in Gethsemane."
"*I* wouldn't have doubted like Thomas."
Please. Where is there proof of that?
Believing in resurrection
metaphorically—that's one thing.
But, when you're struggling
to fathom the loss of one who
owned your heart,
and you're told your beloved is
suddenly, mysteriously alive again,
those words just seem cruel,
especially when your
crucified beloved
was always the one
who did the resurrecting.
Notice, Jesus met Thomas
with compassion, gently using
the disciple's own words
to convince him to believe.
"Put your finger here
and see my hands.
Reach out your hand
and put it in my side."
Those were the words
that made Thomas realize
Jesus had been listening,
that Jesus had been there,
alive, all along.

Now we all get to
fall under the blessing
Jesus breathed that night.
"Blessed are those
who have not seen
and yet have come to believe."
Now, when doubt visits us—
and it will—
Jesus sometimes
whispers our words
back to us as a reminder
that he is listening.
That he is with us.
That he. Is. Alive.

John 20:19–31

Reverence

Like Peter,
we approach the throne
by invitation,
this new trembling in the soul
born of joy, not the terror of old.
How awesome is He
who sits on the throne,
who calls you, me
"Child, Friend, Beloved."
Gone the wretched fear
of a faceless deity,
distant and unknown.
Christ, the Lord
has brought him near.
Forehead to the ground,
I choose to worship the Light.
Reverence comes naturally, now,
even when
the fellowship of suffering
is the price of doing right.

1 Peter 3:13–32

Source

The recipe for joy:
Take one babe, one boy,
who became man.
Not just any babe,
not just any boy.
Not just any man,
but the Son
who made sun and moon
and all we see.
He is the source.
His course is the one
we must sail
to reach happiness.
This voyage,
the sturdy fellow-ship
he steers
as captain of the heart.
Our part—black, brown,
white or otherwise
is to climb aboard,
giving up our "I"
and "me" and "mine"
and leaving behind
hurt and hate
and all that would separate
us from him, who is
the babe, the boy, the man,
the Son, the Savior
the source of all
the happiness and joy
we, together,
can ever hope to know.

1 John 1:1–4

Fool's Errand

Jesus has a penchant for
sending us on odd errands.
Ask the early disciples,
dispatched to a stranger's home
in order to borrow a colt,
this in a culture with
zero tolerance for thieves.
A risky business, at the very least,
especially for followers
who didn't comprehend
the why of it all.
The Lord had a purpose,
of course.
He always does.
But how often are we
let in on the secret?
Every day, the Lord
calls us to tasks
that seem to have
no rhyme or reason,
errands that appear to be
questionable, at best.
Go into the world
and love your enemies.
Put the needs of others
before your own.
Bless those who
despitefully use you.
Forgive the unforgiveable.
Give yourself away.
Strange errands, indeed.
And what do we say? Is there a yes
on the tips of our tongues?

Just as at Bethpage and Bethany,
the Lord understands
the why of his call,
and, in the end, that's all
we really need to know.

Mark 11:1–11

Shadowed Perspective

To follow in the Lord's footsteps
seems a lofty, noble goal
appealing when imagined
as a saccharine, bloodless thing,
the aura of it
emblazoned with glory.
But, a daughter of slaves,
I see this mandate from
a shadowed perspective,
framed within the gaze of the cross,
heard within the echo of curses
spat upon the Lord,
felt against the pounding
stampede of injustice
running Jesus into the ground,
and his only retaliation—silence.
Or harder yet, prayers
for his offenders.
In those moments
however brief, or long, or endless,
when we are cursed, spat upon,
reviled unjustly,
to follow in his footsteps
is a call that galls.
And yet,
the risen Lord reminds us:
If we follow in his footfalls,
even to an ignominious death,
we will be gloriously resurrected
to Life Eternal.

1 Peter 2:19–25

Angel Talk

Angels in the daytime
are anything but routine.
Yet there they were,
reciting the impossible
like old news:
He is risen.
My mind still stuck
on that stone, wondering
who rolled it away.
Were the disciples
stuck on that, too?
Or was it the missing body,
or the eerie way his clothes
were left behind?
Sometimes, we tend
to miss the point.
He. Is. Risen.
Now comes the work
of building his kingdom,
of reflecting his light
through the transformed lives
his bloody sacrifice made possible.
His end, a new beginning.
His death and resurrection,
an arrow pointing us
in a new direction.
Lord, may we, like arrows,
bend ourselves to your touch.
May we fly straight and free
wherever you would send us.

Luke 24:1–12, 1 Corinthians 15:19–26

Holy Architecture

Who of us has never
felt rejected, tossed aside,
ground underfoot
by those who failed
to see our beauty?
Peter reminds us,
we were not the first.
Chips off the old block,
we are called to be like Christ,
living stones, precious to God,
designed to fit into
the body of the temple,
offering our throbbing
broken hearts as mortar for
God's holy architecture—unless
we stubbornly refuse to be used.
What if Joseph had declined to serve
in Potiphar's household?
Or Moses had said,
"I prefer Egypt's bread"
Or Mary had said, "Not me, Lord."
How foolish to refuse to allow
our rough edges to be chiseled smooth
by the Royal Carpenter,
or to decline to be arranged
in the precise order
El Shaddai had in mind from the first.
He, alone, can make of us a mirror
of the light and mercy
this dis–eased world
will surely die without.

1 Peter 2:2–10

Trouble Makers

You know the story:
Paul, Silas, and Luke hit the road,
their plans loosely made.
They submitted to God
and the guidance of the Holy Spirit.
One chapter has them on their way
to the place of prayer when
Paul called out a divining demon
from a slave, who could then no longer
sell predictions for her owners.
Livid, they called down
the power of Rome on the heads
of these troublesome Christ-followers
who neither defended themselves
nor cried out for justice.
Instead, the three surrendered to
whatever God had in mind by
allowing his faithful ones to be beaten
and paraded to prison.
Their throbbing wounds
notwithstanding,
they passed their time in the stocks,
in the drafty darkness,
praying and singing hymns to God,
their love and joy overflowing,
showing the other prisoners
how to truly be free.
And when an earthquake
loosed their chains,
they remained because
God had put them there.

Such actions were a living sermon
the jailer could not deny.
"What must I do to be saved?"
he cried, revealing
the point of it all,
the call to go into the world
and make disciples.

Acts 16:16–34

Woman Calling

In Macedonia, on the Sabbath,
Paul and Silas looked for worshippers
outside the gate—
isn't that often the kind of place
that draws God's attention?
There, they found Lydia and
other women gathered by a river,
the very site where they wash clothes
and God washes hearts,
as he did this particular baptism,
blessing Lydia and her family
to come to him, fully.
But, what if the vision that led
Paul and Silas to Macedonia
had been of a *woman* calling?
Would they have been so earnest
in coming? God knows.
It's just a question.
And who was Paul looking for?
And what did he expect to find,
or to do?
Isn't it true that so much
Kingdom work happens
when we're on the way
to where we imagine
the Lord wants us?
It doesn't really matter,
I suppose,
so long as our hearts
are as open as Lydia's,
ready and waiting for whatever
vision or commission
The Father chooses to send.

Acts 16:9–15

Unvarnished Healing

There are those who insist
gifts of speaking in tongues
and heavenly healing belong
to yesteryear when countless
Holy Spirit movement stories
flowed from that old-time religion.
But were those mighty works of God
merely once-upon-a-time?
According to John, Jesus defined
the "we" of this work, a ministry calling
with no timelines, deadlines,
or gender-limits implied.
I heal, you heal, he/she/we heal
whenever God moves through prayer
and the laying on of hands,
work perfectly modeled and planned
by the Perfect One, himself
on a particular Sabbath,
when his mercy settled on a man
sightless from birth.
Curious, how the disciples'
very first thoughts turned to
whose sin was to blame
for this blindness,
while some Pharisees rebuked
this rule-breaker rabbi for
daring to work on the Sabbath.
Which are we?
Disciples or Pharisees?
Will judgment cause us
to miss the miracle?

We are called to enter into
all of God's good work,
and to worship him
with praise for his
unvarnished healing.

John 9:1–41

Proof

"Show me" was not only
the demand of
Doubting Thomas.
This posture
of the disenchanted,
the discouraged,
is all too common.
Arms firmly folded
across our chests,
we toss out the challenge.
"God is real? The gospel true?
Show me," we say.
And God, who owes us
nothing but disdain
deigns to show us, anyway.
The widow of Zarephath
steps forward
to bear witness, how she,
convinced whatever God that be
had long since forgotten
her and her hungry boy,
experienced the miracle
of unending oil and meal,
and then, saw her son,
stolen by Death,
returned to her, alive again.
Proof enough, I'd say.
But there was also Paul,
or should I say, Saul,
utterly transformed
for all the world to see.
And then, there's you.

And then, there's me,
not what we once were,
nor yet what we will be.
We, with all the saints before,
bear proof of a gospel good,
and true, and powerful.

1 Kings 17:8–24, Galatians 1:11–24

Bones to Pick

Forgive me, but
I have a few bones to pick
with Paul,
not the least of which is
his aggravating admission
that the believer's complete self-control
is only an illusion.
The general gist of his
annoying announcement?
"I don't do what I want to do,
but what I hate.
I'm a prisoner of the law of sin
at work within me."
Thanks a lot!
This malaise seems, let's call it
slightly schizophrenic.
Any takers? No?
(Clearly, he wasn't only
talking about himself.)
Personally, I much prefer
"The devil made me do it,"
a suggestion that
the cause of the sin I commit
comes from without—not within.
It's comfort I'm looking for, Paul,
not proof of some lingering
spiritual disorder
haunting the soul.
Yes, knowing
we are not alone in this
is somewhat soothing, so
grudging gratitude to you for that.

In the end, we know
the gift of grace is not to be
thoroughly under-minded.
Once we bend our wills
to the Father through the Son,
God honors our sincere confession
with deliverance—over, and over,
and over again,
never once rescinded,
no matter the tug-of-war
that besets us
as we wrestle between
sin's entanglement
and our sweet, sweet delight
in the law of the Lord.

Romans 7:15–25

Dark Torches

News of another cross-burning
singes my heart,
paralyzing me where I sit.
I drink my tears and read
"God is light, and in him
there is no darkness at all,"
and I wonder
how many of the deceived,
professing Christ this time,
lifted their torches in unison?
How many made
of no consequence
Christ's death on the cross
for me? How many polluted
this symbol of Life
to threaten the death
of my people?
Jesus weeps, I am certain,
though he does not
spin in his grave
but only because—
Thank God—
he isn't in it!
And so, in spite of all,
I sing Hallelujah!
Despite the revival of
lynchings in this land,
and sanctioned shootings
past numbering,
I can continue to pray

"Lord, have mercy,"
because the heat of his
pure, good light
will one day burn
every remnant of injustice
to ash.
Good Lord,
may we be filled
with your righteous fire.
Bless us to be vessels
of your undiminished Light.
Help the true church
burn bright for you.

1 John 1:5–2:2

The Problem of Evil

God's word
never shies away from
the topic of hardship
or evil in the world.
"For your sake," we read,
"we are being killed
all day long,
accounted as sheep
to be slaughtered."
We gasp, then
shake off this truth,
it being both painful
and inconvenient,
then we go back
to our daily lives
in which our egos
strut proudly
feigning invincibility.
Still, God's word blatantly
reveals the weaknesses
of the world and the soul
in graphic detail.
Deny, deny, deny
the enemy whispers
and we're quite inclined to
because we're most vulnerable
in our weakness,
and who wants that?
Yet the proof resides
in our own bodies
hidden in the thicket
of memory.

Wordless, we sometimes
shiver for reasons
we don't even know,
but the Spirit does,
and delivers us a promise
(made and kept)
to rescue us
in our weakness,
to strengthen, uplift,
empower, and intercede.
When we can't speak,
it doesn't matter.
The Spirit speaks for us,
translates our voiceless groans
so the Lord
can hear them
and dispel our fears.
If God is for us,
who can be against us?
This is the serum the world
has waited for,
the antidote to all fear—
and we are blessed
to have it.

Romans 8:26–39

SUMMER

Wading In

How often do we
wade into the Word
and thrash around,
weighed down by
indecision,
in desperate search
of the Father's
will for us.
And yet, His will
is less mystery
than we imagine.
He has made us
a chosen race,
a royal priesthood,
a holy nation
for this one purpose:
to proclaim His might,
his glory,
his worthy work
in placing each
living stone of us
precisely where
we need to be
to best reflect
the light
of the Lord.

1 Peter 2:1–10

Greed

The land lay prostrate
so we take advantage
seeding, sowing, plowing
fracking, drilling round the clock
ignoring God's design that we
occupy the land gifted
as grateful caretakers
sharing the wealth
of the harvest
six years running,
then granting the land
a well-earned time off
for rest and replenishment.
A generous arrangement,
but our greed got in the way.
Now we stuff parcels of land
that isn't ours to begin with
into our bottomless pockets
to sell to the highest bidders,
to be used however they choose
because—well—we don't care
about the gift or the giver.
"And what rest?" we say.
"Jubilee is for suckers."
So the overworked earth groans
and too many of her people
limp through life hungry
for there are no grapes left
to glean, and all because
God's good plan
didn't feed our greed.

Leviticus 25:1–5, 23–24

Infinite Surprise

We take God for granted,
assume he will work according to
our ill-informed dictates?
Assumptions are easy, but
they're frequently a mistake.
Remember the Triumphal Entry,
the expectation that King Jesus
would wipe out Rome
with a mighty wave of power,
and inaugurate a newer, kinder
earthly kingdom.
Of course, Messiah
had something else in mind,
and the crowd's Hosannas,
boisterous as they were
and smattered with blessings,
merely paved the way
for disappointment.
Wailing waited in the wings.
Assuming had blinded them
to the truth of the moment:
The triumphal entry
did not mark
the beginning of the end for Rome,
but the end of the beginning
of God's Kingdom,
one not of this world, at all,
but of the heart.
So, come Lord Jesus,
you of infinite surprises.
Take your seat
on the throne
of our lives.

Mark 11:1–11

Daily Delusions

In every day that ends with "y"
we surrender to the illusion of control,
stack our plans like bricks
we mortar together
with the spit of our own egos.
"We will do thus and so, "
we cleverly surmise
as if the future outcome
is solid as cement
and not immune to
any manner of wrecking ball
life might surprise us with.
Setting uncomfortable
truths aside, we lay out
our intentions for the day.
Pretend we are fisher-folk:
"Let's go fishing," we say.
And after our luckless night,
Jesus nudges us to
acknowledge our failure
so that we will be in a place to ask—
and receive—his help.
"You have no fish, have you?
Cast the net on the right side,"
he coaxes. *Again?*
We mutter in our minds,
forgetting God can hear us.
Still, obedience seems
the only sure path to success.
We cast the net and are rewarded—
153 fish! And no, the net does not break.
God is quite capable of containing
every blessing he intends.

Dragging our gilled gifts ashore,
there Jesus stands inviting us, as always,
to come and dine,
the table, as it were, already set with bread.
Jesus loves to show his hand,
ever so subtly—or not: I mean,
153 fish, ya'll! Come. On!
Who is this God?
He. Is. Ours.
When will we learn
to begin each day
with the only one whose plans
cannot be undone?

John 21:1–14

Waiting for the Word

Thanks to Ezra,
we're reminded
how good it is to retreat
for a few precious hours,
to feel God's Glory
rise from his word
like a fine mist
kissing our souls,
wrapping us in a cloud
of grace and truth
that makes us weep
like the people
of Nehemiah's time.
They grew weak from
standing long,
listening to scripture,
interpretation,
and prophecies of
the Promised One.
And now,
owners of this legacy,
we hear the
Word-made-flesh
speak to us, whether in
a still, small voice,
or one like thunder,
and like the people of old,
we tremble,
lift our hands in praise,
bow in prayer and adoration,

on a Sabbath declared holy,
and wait, hungry
for the word the Lord
will bring to light today
so that we can take it
out into the world
for its own good.

Nehemiah 8:1–10, Luke 4:14–21

Divine Adventure

Kings are rarely to be trusted,
as history teaches,
especially the newly crowned.
Perhaps that's why King Jesus
left his royal raiment behind.
But king he was, and is,
and he comes to us
with healing and
a new kingdom in his hand,
eager enough to share it
that he would dare trade
the familiarity of Nazareth
for Capernaum, a new city
where the new country
of a new kingdom
would be revealed.
"The kingdom of heaven
is near," he said, the light of it
shining from his eyes.
Who could resist
the divine adventure?
"Come! Leave your nets.
Follow me."
Jesus knew all about leaving,
and the sadness of goodbye.
He left his heavenly Father's side,
left his earthly home,
left his mother Mary longing for
the smooth and steady sound
of her son's carpentry tools.
Jesus wasn't asking anything
he hadn't done, himself.

Somehow, Peter and Andrew,
James and John
sensed the truth of that.
And like them,
our hearts felt the tug
of this God-man's calling.
And how could we say no?
So, we began the journey
from darkness to kingdom's light,
entering a realm where
hope is solid as stone
and the vocabulary of grace
is spoken daily.
We enter at the Lord's urging,
wondering what country
our new king
will lead us to next.

Matthew 4:12–25

Haiti

In Haiti,
I once did the dirty work
of slathering
wet cement on bricks,
then stacked them
upon a foundation
someone else had laid.
By and by, my friends and I
built what we mistook
for a church.
But that is something
only God can construct.
Remember that old game?
Here's the door.
Here's the steeple.
Here's the church.
Where are the people?
The temple is a
spiritual architecture
assembled from all our
broken pieces.
And yes. It takes
a master's hand.
Beatitudes and holy living
shape us into
the righteous bricks required
as we show mercy,
give to beggars,
become peacemakers,
lend like we mean it,
and love our enemies.
It's simple, really.

We just need to be perfect
like the Father.
Then, we will fit firmly together
upon the sturdy foundation
the Lord became for us
on Calvary's tree.

1 Corinthians 3:10–11, 16–23, Matthew 5:38–48

High Style

Louboutin stillettos
are recognizable at a distance.
Those shiny red soles
tell you everything.
When Gucci handbags
are in a room,
they virtually shout.
Now, I'm not much for labels,
but I've noticed how
God's garments stand out.
Take the suit, a second skin
made of holiness—a rare fabric,
that usually itches, at first
until the wearer
gets used to it;
Beyond that,
God's personal style
is all about the layered look:
the silk of compassion,
golden threads of kindness
woven through the vest,
humility cinching in the waist,
meekness and patience
falling to the ankles,
and love thickly draped
across the shoulders.
The clothing God designs
is never mistaken
for anyone's but his.

And when we're wise enough
to don his attire,
we look like more
than a million.

Colossians 3:12–17

Fish Fry

Jesus came, full-blooded
in his humanity,
impish grin,
a sparkle in his eye,
whispering in our ears
and spinning stories
by the fire after a fish fry.
Why?
So we would know him,
recognize the particular
timbre of his voice,
see him adorned with
true love's piercings,
alive to us and for us
after death failed
to snare him for good—
him a perfect picture
of the life eternal he promised.
He came to tell us we are his,
to invite our cries for healing, help,
comfort, strength.
He came stubborn in his compassion,
fearless in his passion for what is right,
for the words of his Father.
He came to teach us
the alchemy of prayer,
to remind us of the importance
of intercession, assuring us that
God is listening and manifesting
our deepest needs.
He came so we could
tell the difference between

the Prince of Peace
and the prince of the air,
between the first begotten Son
and the Evil one
who has temporary run
of this world.
He came to introduce himself
as the source of everything,
and to let us know
that we who love him
will see him again,
soon and very soon.

1 John 5:13–21

Road Trip

Sometimes,
the route of our blessing
seems serpentine
when we'd rather
the path be direct.
Naaman knew.
Seven marked
the mystical number
of his miraculous healing.
From servant, to wife,
to Naaman, to king,
to king, to prophet, to river.
Now tell me,
wouldn't you have been
slightly miffed by then?
It wasn't merely pride
that Naaman displayed
at the gate of Elisha.
It was—you know,
that little thing
we all wrestle with
from day to day—Frustration.
And the final lesson
Naaman learned,
to heed God's word to the end,
stood as a testament
later spoken of by the One,
by Jesus, a lesson basic to
God's curriculum for us all:
stay faithful, follow through
on whatever instructions
the Lord lays out for us,

step into the rivers
he leads us to
so that we may one day
be a testimony.

2 Kings 5:1–14, Luke 4:16–30

On the Way

Unlike David,
I've never been much
for wilderness excursions,
but I'm intimately familiar with caves,
those pitch-black places of the soul
where no light falls, knife-like,
to carve a human path.
Instead, I'm left
to stumble forward,
nerves and muscles clenching
at the skitter of rats,
and the otherworldly screech
of bats passing through.
Bone-tired and hungry,
I want for water—until you come
bringing your eternal spring,
offering your body as the one meal
I never knew I needed.
And suddenly,
deep down in the darkness,
your brightness breaks through,
illuminating a path to the surface.
I meet widows on the way,
orphans and others poor as me,
and as we slowly ascend,
I share the bread and
the heavenly water
you provided.

Psalm 142

Summer Blockbuster

I'm drawn to stories
of superheroes,
men and women fortified
with special gifts who willingly
bend them toward the service
of humankind.
Each power manifested
is unique, but none
more valuable than the next.
My latest fascination,
if you must know,
is Aqua Man,
a reluctant bridge
between sea and land.
Trident in hand,
he's recognized as King,
and when he summons
the creatures of the deep,
they all follow to do his bidding.
Do we?
When our Christ calls,
do we, with our myriad,
individual, God-selected gifts,
gather to serve the one body
he has fitted us to?
Or do we somehow
imagine his body to be plural?
Seahorse, seal, shark, humpback—
the shape and nuance of our gifts
vary according to Celestial purpose,
but the spiritual ocean
we all swim in, by God's grace,
is One.

1 Corinthians 12:1–11

Renovation

God has a penchant
for fixer-uppers,
we human houses with
peeling paint,
rusted pipes,
cracked shingles,
faulty wiring
and shoddy foundations
desperately in need
of reconstruction.
No point in us
beating our chests,
or patting ourselves
on the back
after Christ is done
renovating our souls.
He's the one
who gets credit for
making us beautiful.
Don't forget,
we started off
poor in spirit,
meek and mourning,
parched and panting.
Before we could
even imagine
inheriting the earth,
we had to sink
low enough
to comprehend
the wisdom
of looking up.

Once we did,
we found the Lord
waiting and ready to make
our fleshly houses suitable
for his habitation,
and his gift of joy.

1 Corinthians 1:18–31, Matthew 5:1–12

Relentless

Perseverance furthers
is the motto
stitched into my skin
since birth.
And yes, I was
a stubborn tot.
Call it a blessing. Or not.
For now, just picture
a little one,
endlessly tugging
his mother's skirt
like a bell he's intent
on ringing.
Annoying,
from one perspective.
From another,
it's rather cute.
Either way,
nothing distracts,
or dissuades the child
from his pursuit.
You see the lesson, here.
The child balls
his small twin fists,
persistence and perseverance,
then single-mindedly
pursues whatever he's after.
Likewise, when we
call on the Lord,
we need to knock
on heaven's door
like a child,

knowing all the while,
the Hallowed One
is on the other side,
waiting with
good gifts
in abundance.

Luke 11:1–13

Potter's Business

Who is the Potter
and who is the Clay?
Does the outcome depend
on the hour? The day?
Does faithfulness—
or the lack—force
the Great Potter's hand?
Will he crush or caress?
Will the clay understand?
Will the clay see the joy
mixed with love
and with tears
that water the Potter's eye
through the years,
as he labors to fashion
his original design,
the glorious vessel
that he had in mind?
Will the final result be
a beautiful, elegant pot,
one that is useful
or one that is not?
Whatever the outcome—
whole, chipped,
fragmented shards,
the process is dreadfully,
painfully hard.
It's best if we follow
the Potter's great plan,
for we are the clay
in the Almighty's hand.

Jeremiah 18:1–11

Clever Choices

Friends are golden, unless they're not. "Choose your friends carefully," loving parents often say, and we repay them with sarcasm, a shrug, or a smirk, because what do they know?

Plenty, if Solomon is to be believed. Heeding the instructions of our elders is on his checklist for wisdom and the good life. Choose each companion well, and here's how to tell when

you haven't: said friend will crook the finger and invite you to follow down an enticing rabbit hole of evil. Oh, you may miss the knife in the friend's pocket, the scent of blood at the end of

the journey, but you'll pick up this common litany: the quick-fix, the easy answer, the promise of something for nothing, a feast of sweetness purchased with the thinnest slice of something sour.

Danger, Will Robinson! Cross the street! Walk the other way! Stay on the side of those who fear God—the place where wisdom begins. Brush up on righteousness, justice, equity.

God has the key to all the insightful words and riddles found in his wisdom book. If we want that key, all we need do is ask.

Proverbs 1:1–17

Pursuit of Peace

Serving God is never
a passive profession.
Resisting the Devil
is only half the equation.
The other half
is doing good.
Seeking peace
is equally complex.
I love the serenity
of waves lapping the shore,
but the enjoyment of it
is miles from my front door,
and the hot drive to reach it
promises to be
neither quiet nor peaceful.
A beautiful relationship,
between people or nations,
is something exquisite to desire,
but it frequently requires
acts of forgiveness and apology.
Neither comes easily.
Peace demands work, strategy.
We have to be in hard pursuit.
Sometimes it feels
impossible to know
where to start, unless
we begin with the heart of God,
with the fear of the Lord
after which
everything is possible.

Psalm 34:11–14

Looking for the Exit

Each soul created is unique,
but as Solomon reminds us,
there is nothing new
under the sun.
Wars and rumors of wars
come upon each generation.
Bad news pounds us
like water on rock
and the fear of drowning
threatens to take us under.
Floods invade our cities,
rushing through the streets
of our minds, like trouble.
We trip over the rubble
left in the wake of fire, earthquake,
hurricane, and tornado,
and for a moment, all seems lost.
But our wilderness is less wild
with you in it, Lord.
You are the river in our desert.
In the midst of this,
or any time of calamity,
you promise something new
and on that truth,
we stand to praise you.

Isaiah 43:15–21

Broken

On a day most blessed, we say yes to Christ,
making space for him in the small, spare room

of our hearts, never guessing how he will
enlarge it with his light and the love of saints

who look suspiciously like you. Love's true
language is a translation unexpected. One heart

breaks in the body, and tears spring from another's
eyes. One belly, hollow and howling with hunger

makes another's stomach growl. One fractures
an ankle, and another swells with sympathy, offers

helping hands and healthy feet, or bends the back
to prune another's roses, or makes a meal for someone

else to eat. I have seen through Paul's eyes and my own
the love of the saints for one another. The love of Christ,

and God's refining fire, burns and burnishes the Body
golden. No wonder Paul speaks of riches and glorious

inheritance among the saints. "I do not cease to give
thanks for you," says Paul. Say I. And thanks is due,

indeed, for the gift of sanctified community—purchased
once and for all by the One broken body, pierced for us.

Ephesians 1:15–23

Noah Spins

Noah spins this particular origin story,
how long before Kermit the Frog intoned
the Rainbow Connection, or the LBGTQ

community flew the colors as its flag, God
tied the rainbow round the cloudy finger of
sky to remind himself of his sacred oath

of mercy toward humankind, the earth
and all things living. Covenant is now
become the C-word we sin-inclined embrace

gratefully—especially when we're desperate
for reassurance. No more water. The fire next
time is how James Baldwin put it, right? Yet

we often find ourselves in leaky canoes, adrift
amidst our personal, self-made floods, with
wildfires raging all around. We'd surely burn,

or drown were it not for the buoy of belief, the
life-saving tether of covenant held steady by the
sturdy hand of God pulling us safely back to

redemption's shore, to catch another breath of
forgiveness, to begin again—once more.

Genesis 9:8–17

FALL

Imaginary Numbers

I never understood the point
of imaginary numbers.
If they don't exist,
why am I required to do
anything with them?
It all makes zero sense to me,
So I'm not going to be the one
balancing the church books,
or working through
intricate plans
for renovations
to the square inch.
And don't even talk
about tech.
I'm currently driving a car
that's smarter than
I asked for.
My learning curve
is so steep,
I'll never reach the top.
So don't call on me
to run the soundboard,
or check that the song lyrics
make it up on the screen.
And, for the record,
I don't make coffee
or teach Sunday school,
but if you need a poem,
I'm your girl.
Of course, spiritual gifts
are different from talents,
but in one way,
they're the same:

We all do what we can
and the kingdom
is better for it.

1 Corinthians 12:12–31

Particular Perfection

Glass art always
gets me drooling.
Practiced discipline
is all that keeps
my itchy fingers planted
deep inside my pockets
as I tour a glass art gallery
or museum.
"Don't touch," say the signs
as if someone knows
I'll be sorely tempted.
But should I slip,
my failure is not likely
to lead to my death.
I'll bet the Levites
would've liked
to trade places.
Given the task to
relocate the tabernacle
and all its Holy contents,
God's warning was clear:
Touch anything, and you'll die.
Whew! The thought, alone,
is enough to
make me shudder,
so I'd rather concentrate
on the particulars,
how each tool,
each covering fabric,
each color, each order of task
was specifically assigned,
reminding us that
our infinitely kind,

generous, merciful Father
can also be wholly exacting,
and we'd be wise
to heed his instructions—
especially in the wilderness.

Numbers 4:1–20

Hold Hope

Now faith is the substance
of things hoped for,
the evidence of things unseen.
A bit forensic, isn't it,
this talk of evidence?
But it does seem fitting.
The DNA of hope is faith,
the very stuff on which
my hope, your hope,
our hope is based.
Just trace the evidence
and you'll find the proof
of good, of God, of
all things invisible,
like the face of The Father,
his work in our midst,
the angels he dispatches
time and again,
discerning when and
where they're needed.
We need to step out
on that which
is proven certain,
hold Hope like the
eternal rope of faith
it's made from.
Why call it a leap
when you know who
controls the landing?
God has already
set the markings,
poured the concrete
of his own convictions.

All we have to *do*
is walk, run—or leap
where he tells us to.

Hebrews 11

Words and Will

The daily to-do list screams from an imaginary
refrigerator door: "Each of you, remember to do

your chores. In me abide. Hide your heart from
the love of this world. Nestle, instead, in my words

and will. Cling to Christ's instruction. Know which
brother and sister is true. Not everyone who says

they are mine belongs. Some are familiar, but are not
family. Beware of the antichrists among us yesterday,

today, and tomorrow. My great sorrow is, some may
yet be deceived. Fathers, sons, sisters, brothers, those

who are anointed, embrace my Spirit and one another.
My firstborn will be back, soon. There's food in the

fridge. Don't I always provide? Now, remember:
Abide. Do your homework, and live forever.

Signed, Your Dad"

1 John 2:12–27

Jenga

Game Night is anathema, to me.
Quite simply, I'm the world's
sorest loser. As a child,
the only way my mother could
rope me into her favorite game
—gin rummy—
was by promising to throw
a few good hands my way.
It didn't matter that the win
was meaningless.
A win was all I wanted.
Of course, not all game results
can be, shall we say, pre-arranged.
Beg all you want,
no player can hand you the win
in Monopoly or, let's say, Jenga.
But we are not here to discuss games.
Today's topic is Resurrection.
No connection, really, except for this:
Remove resurrection
like a Jenga piece,
and the whole Church of Christ
would tumble.
No one scores in that game.
But Praise God,
Christ, our Cornerstone,
did rise from the dead,
and no game, or gamer,
can undo it.

1 Corinthians 15:12–20

Eden Tells Us

Eden tells us
God is partial to gardens,
to displaying his love
in the face of a flower.
The Creator of giants,
God himself
treads the earth tenderly.
Why not we?
Why not choose
bipedal motion
or bicycle over
the standard vehicle
belching poison
into the air?
Why should we care,
you wonder?
Our Heavenly Father
asks us to follow
in his footsteps.
He has always known
how to love the earth,
how to tuck his creatures
in for the night,
how to fill their bellies.
He has modeled
what it means
to watch over raven,
magpie, sparrow.
Man.
God, himself,
has shown us how.

Now, all that remains
is that each,
in his or her own way
say, "Yes, Lord."

Genesis 1:20–31

Sound the Trumpet

On certain days we meet the dawn,
gasp at the beauty of the sun
splintering the darkness.
"Look!" we say to anyone around.
Occasionally,
sunsets steal our attention
glorious in a wild prism of color.
"Look!" we tell others
because keeping such beauty
to ourselves would be a sin.
But what about
that good pure light
from which all others derive?
The Son enters our orbit,
hands and feet adorned with
the wounds of love,
his very being
radiance personified.
Will we not say, "Look!"
to those far and near?
Or do we believe our witness
to be unnecessary?
John received the calling,
first to beat the drum
and point to the Radiant One.
Consider this:
the magnificent Milky Way
drenches the night sky with light.
And yet, there are many who miss it.
We don't always see
what we're not looking for.

John, made witness to the Light,
pointed the way for all
willing to look.
Can we do any less?

John 1:6–8, 19–28

Neighborly

Leave it to a lawyer
to ask Jesus to define
the word "neighbor"—
not that we're any better.
Like the legal eagle in Luke
who thought himself clever,
we long for
an easy check-list
of dos and don'ts
and simple definitions
that limit the number
of good deeds we need
to concern ourselves with.
Why worry our little heads
about helping everyone
who requires assistance
when we can narrow
the sum total of neighbors
we reach out to?
Mind you, we're all for
being good Samaritans—
up to a point.
But we are not called
to be stingy with grace.
That's not what was
modeled for us.
Or do we,
even for a minute
imagine that
Jesus asked the Father
"Exactly which sinners
should I die for?"

Luke 10:25–37

In Search of Wiggle Room

Ah, the Law! The comfort of the
legal list is gone. Immediately,
we miss the narrow confines,

finding we can no longer hide
behind simple dos and don'ts.
Jesus, not quite so meek and mild,

has come to change the game,
introducing different weapons for
a deeper war against sin. He rips

the veil off our limited understanding,
leaves naked the nuanced, broader, harder
marching orders our God intends. There's

no room now for hatred of our enemies.
Deep and guttural prayer for their well-
being is the mandate replacing hate. An

oath of any kind by Christian soldiers
purchases as much hell as a lie. In this
spiritual war more fully revealed, lust

of the eye is deemed as sinful as adultery.
Where's the wiggle room in that? "Gone,"
says God. "I mean it when I say you must

be holy as I am holy, perfect in every way!"
What? Really, Lord? But, how? Ah! That's
the open secret, isn't it? At ease, soldier.

You can do nothing of your own, but,
with God—yes. Now you understand
the rest.

Matthew 5:17–48, 2 Corinthians 10:4–5

Flip the Switch

Puny as we are,
we beloved sons and daughters
have it in us to grieve the Spirit,
our faithlessness a frustration
to the God of all power.
Consider how our doubt
short-circuits blessings
flowing our way.
How often do we miss out?
The original twelve walked
right alongside God's Son
yet sometimes found
their own faith on life support.
Failing to free a young epileptic
of a demon, the disciples
pulled the Lord aside to ask why.
"Little Faith" was his painful reply.
The Father's power is never
diminished by human doubt,
but ours is. Daily, we must
remember to pray, full-hearted,
remember to, as they say,
check for loose cable connections,
make sure our fragile faith
is plugged into
the source of holiness and might.
Then, all we need do
is flip the switch and wait
for the light.

Matthew 17:14–21

Conflicting Comforts

Our self-named towers
tell us we're the enlightened few.
We line the walls of our world
with possessions that promise to
reflect who we really are.
But they're fun-house mirrors,
masking the dark, casting
false images of ourselves
as giants in the land,
impervious to pain.
Blind to our selfishness and
poverty of spirit, we often
strut along our paved streets
naked as that storybook emperor,
wondering why we feel a draft.
Should we look to Laodicea,
we'd know that's far from God's
design or desire.
If we turn to him daily, listen closely
for his knock upon the doors
of our hearts, and fling them wide,
he'll clothe us in robes
of righteousness,
show us our true selves
in the mirror of his love,
offer us gold refined by fire;
he'll fit us for his kingdom, and
a place beside him on his throne
in the Empire of Light
that will last
forever.

Revelation 3:14–22

The Real

The dark fantasy of Star Wars
seems the spawn of the real:
the prophecy of suffering,

sun and moon blackened,
and the sudden departure of
Celestial bodies—desperation

would undo us all if that were
the end of the story. But in the
middle of Earth's darkness,

at the center of the abyss, God
strikes the match of hope and
lights the candle within us with

this truth: *He is coming!* So, the
heart's cycle begins: First comes
the knowing, then excitement fans

the flame. Time passes, but the
yearning remains. More time passes
and impatience rears its head. And

just as bone-shaking groans threaten
to rip the soul in two, we hear that whisper,
anew: *He is coming!* So, the heart cycle

begins again. And what of the in-between?
The liminal space where darkness abides
for a season? That is what the hope is for—
until He comes.

Mark 13:24–37

Sturdy Steed

His name is Light,
is Immanuel, is Hope
Another school shooting.
Oh, my God, Julia. Julia!
I know that kid!
He lives two streets over,
down by Pine Cone,
where the new Miguel's
just opened.
You know, right past
Hope, a sturdy—wait
Wait! *Wait!* Doc!
Give me a minute, okay?
Jesus H. Christ!
What—What the hell are
we talking about here?
Last appointment, you said
I was right as rain, and now...
"I'm sorry Keith."
Yeah, yeah. Well...
Give it to me straight.
How serious is Hope,
a sturdy steed takes us—wait
Oh, that's rich. Hah.
Guess you been hittin'
a little too much eggnog, Stew!
What. What? You gotta be joking.
Tell me you're joking, Stew. Stew?
Stew. Stew! Fired? Fired?
Right before Christmas.
Hope, a sturdy steed takes us
Get off of me, Mom! I hate you!

Rachel, please. Can't we just—
Don't touch me! I hate you! I...
Hope, a sturdy steed takes us far
if only we remember
to mount up and ride.

Romans 8:18–25

Ambush

Trouble, skilled at ambush,
waits for us round every corner,
certain as sunrise. Our eyes may
have adjusted to this world of
darkness, but not our hearts.

Those tender places in us pulse with
the pain of poverty, illness, injustice,
loneliness and loss. Famine, earthquake,
mudslide, war—Is there no end? The
question echoes through the ages.

Isaiah heard it and answered with the
quintessential "God said." And the word
was "Yes," offered by the Promise Keeper,
the same who promised, and sent, the voice
of one crying in the wilderness, "Prepare ye

the way of the Lord"; the same who promised,
and sent, the Messiah born in Bethlehem.
Trustworthy is his name. "Be anxious for
nothing," he whispers. Are we listening?
We are in the good, strong hands of the Lord.

Mark 1:1–8, 2 Peter 3:8–15

Reputation

Reputation is no small thing.
How we are seen
in the eyes of others
can sting, or soothe—
depending.
Whether we waltz,
stumble, strut or sashay
down life's runway,
loyalty and faithfulness
are tattoos neither man
nor God can miss.
And while we're
on the subject
of being seen,
forget haute-couture.
Be adorned, instead,
with trust in Yahweh.
Speak or shout his name
with reverence,
look askance at evil,
be wise enough
to choose his limitless
all-knowingness
over the tiny teacup
half-full of human
musings amassed in life's
blink-of-an-eye—
Do this, and that slim seam
where flesh meets soul
will be blessed to know
healing and renewal

time, and time,
and time again—
not according to
the math of men,
but of God.

Proverbs 3:3–8

Scarred Service

Witness to their master's crucifixion
and freshly scarred from beatings
within the walls of prison
and without, the disciples discerned
that they preached the gospel
on borrowed time, to whit
their minds and hearts were devoted
to the task of winning souls.
So what to do when
foul charges were brought
that believing widows and orphans
of the outsider, Greek-speaking
Jewish contingent
were receiving less food and grain
than other widows and orphans
among them?
Clearly, the Lord weighed
each vulnerable person worthy
of equal love and care.
And yet, the twelve dare not
set aside preaching and teaching
to monitor daily food distribution.
In search of a prayerful solution,
all the disciples were gathered together.
Seven men were selected and anointed
to oversee the fair distribution of goods
to those among them on the margins.
Lest you imagine this service was,
for an instant, considered frivolous,
keep in mind: those called to it
were filled with the Holy Spirit,
and revered for integrity and wisdom—

Only the best of the best
to answer God's call to serve—
a call no less lofty than
the spreading of God's word.

Acts 6:1–7

Zacchaeus

What would you do
to see Jesus?
Climb a sycamore tree?
Swim across a vast sea?
Share your wealth
with the poor?
Dare to open the door
to your home,
to your heart?
Promise the Lord
that you're ready to start
down a path seeking
God's own glory?
That is the story
we're created to tell.
Would you, like Zacchaeus
admit that your soul
is riddled with sin, then
embrace the chance offered
to begin life again?
What would you do to fall
under God's grace?
Would you wet the Lord's feet
with the tears from your eyes?
Choose that which is true
and repent of all lies?
Would you follow him into
the shadow of night,
risk seasons of wilderness
to be near his light?

Did your love for Jesus
begin at first sight?
Tell me, what did *you* do
to see him?

Luke 19:1–10

Abide

As a child,
I found the visit of angels
a comfort, their company lit
with joy and laughter.
Then again, they never delivered
disturbing news.
A baby? Planted in me
as a virgin?
Up comes the specter
of Joseph's tortured expression
as he imagines betrayal,
the menacing prospect of
the Nazareth gossip mill,
and the certain threat
of stoning.
Who would call this
"Good news?"
Yet, there are moments
the Heavenly Father wraps us in
the sturdy embrace of his peace,
then calls us to tasks impossible,
and we, like Mary, are
able to answer, "Yes, Lord."
All that's required is that we
abide in the strength
of His embrace.

Luke 1:26–38

Attentive

Stay tuned! Stay alert!
You'd better watch out!
He knows when you are sleeping.
He knows when—you've sung the song.
Sounds like Santa has ripped a page
from the Word, doesn't it?
But Old St. Nick is talking about
presents in the present,
not the gift of life eternal.
Santa, no matter how jolly,
is not the reason for joy,
or why we need to be alert.
Nor do we wait for the Lord's
first appearance.
It's His second coming
we look forward to, the dream
of ultimate deliverance,
light shattering darkness
once and for all.
It's the promise of God's
forever presence
we dare not miss.
It's the "not yet—but almost"
we hold dear.
The when of it all escapes us.
So, what's the point
of living like Christ is,
once again, about to appear,
like he's almost here?
The attentive waiting
gently goads us to good works,
helps us to strive to be holy—
right now.

Mark 13:24–37

To Hear Paul Tell It

To hear Paul tell it,
David's seed was
more prolific than he knew.
From him descended
the multiplicity of One:
Wellspring of holiness,
fount of grace,
Prince of Peace,
Conqueror of Death,
Blessed Redeemer,
he who carried
a certificate of
authenticity
written in his blood;
he whose name
is Emmanuel.
Who else was born
of God and a virgin?
(Thanks to the Angel,
Joseph was in
on the secret.)
Paul declared
the Lordship of Jesus
with a casual nod
to his power.
Of course,
one who raises the dead
requires no fanfare
or Hollywood treatment,
only obedience
from the beloved
We, who praise him
for all of the above.

Romans 1:1–7, Matthew 1:18–25

Whatever

In this "whatever" generation,
contracts have all but
lost their meaning. They are
flimsy things to lose, to shred,
to flippantly ignore, or break.
We love the loophole,
and hate the fine print,
unless it serves us.
Meticulously composed contracts
are rarely read before they're signed.
The giveaway is always
the blank stare or, Huh? What?
whenever I raise some salient point
clearly stated therein.
But that response won't work
in the courts of heaven.
God is old school. His contract
cannot be lost, or shredded.
Ignore or break the particulars
at your own risk.
(Don't lie. Don't steal.
Don't neglect to keep
all ten commandments,
or else...)
Sign this agreement?
Yes! Nevertheless,
one warning:
it's useless to look
for loopholes.
And yet, lest we forget,

God's contract
is a living organism
unlike any we've ever seen.
It's amended by Grace—*Grace*,
complete with
a new bill of rights
for the redeemed,
giving the forgiven a free pass
into the Holy of Holies,
granting us direct access to
the King of kings.
And the old law?
Perfectly fulfilled
by the only one
who could.
God's contract,
God's covenant
is good.

Exodus 20:1–17

Our Hunger Satisfied

Shall I tell you
about Elisha,
a servant who knew well
how to spell "loyal"?
He clung to his master, Elijah,
hungry to minister
alongside him
until the moment
Jehovah's whirlwind
would come to steal him away.
Elisha knew the master's
leave-taking was imminent,
and knowing, chose to practice
the gift of presence—not eyeing
future blessings, or battles,
nor lost in reminiscences.
This disciple chose to serve
and follow his teacher wherever
he roamed, echoing sentiments
from the lips of Ruth:
"Wherever you go, I will go."
And his reward?
Elisha witnessed
the parting of the Jordan,
felt the mantle of his master,
laced with the power
of God, grace his
own shoulders, received
the double portion of
spirit he hungered for most.
It would seem a satisfying thing
to practice being present,

to labor and rest
in the time called Now,
in the place called Here,
with the Lord.

2 Kings 2:1–12

WINTER

Strength Is Ours

Locked in the prisons of our
daily limitations,
we often have cause to wonder
what Godly good can come from us.
How can we, in our
sometimes shriveled state,
hope to rise to live lives of devotion?
But Paul reminds believers,
despite any adverse circumstance,
our marching orders remain intact:
Sing. Shout. Proclaim. Praise.
The where of it hardly matters because
the Lord is always Emmanuel,
the Word made alive, forever present,
his weapons, and ours, in hand:
Grace. Truth. And all the love
we'll ever need.
Jeremiah tells us a life of radiance
awaits, a time of joy
on the heels of mourning.
Strength is ours for the asking,
and with it, power from
the God of comfort and peace,
who paints our tomorrows
with Light.

Ephesians 1:3–14, John 1:1–18, Jeremiah 31:7–14

Word

Word. Words matter, which
is why we grasp at them daily,
suffering frustration when
the right one refuses to come.

Word. We give it as a promise,
though not always kept. We revel
at those whose fingers elegantly
dance through the air translating
spoken word into signs for the deaf.

Word. We marvel at the way
language houses the nuances of
its nation, enshrines whatever that
culture deems most holy or even
hides the punch lines of its jokes.

Word. How often are we reminded
to take care what words we use,
what words we choose, marking
their power? Yet, we have long lost
our reverence for words.

We fling them thoughtlessly like
feathers—or stones, forgetting that
all that is, and was, and ever will be
was born of the word, which is
the life, which is the light.

We need reminders, witnesses
like John who can testify of the
Word most holy, most light-filled,
most mysterious. The Word,
John tells us, begins every story.

There is no once-upon-a-time without him—
no Advent until he walked the earth,
wrapped in skin, his light overcoming
the darkness that presses in. And what
has this Word to do with us?

Only everything, says John. To all who
received him, who believed in his name,
he gave power to become children of God.
Is that not reason enough for reverence?

John 1:1–15

Weaponry

How casually do we
wield our words,
those emblems of power
which are mightier than?
A word can
dress our thoughts,
capture our emotions,
encourage, inspire, elevate,
and move us to tears.
A word can also bind, blind,
diminish or destroy
with a single blow.
A mighty thing, I've seen a word
walk right off the page.
One even left the stage of heaven
to become flesh.
But did we listen to him
when he spoke?
Do we listen, now?
How can we ever hope to dine on
God's good and plenty
if we don't first receive the Word
who invited us to the table?
I know: it's all something of a riddle:
a word radiant with life and light
who moves on legs and feet
and has a heart that beats for
the humankind he made and loved
beyond his dying breath.
But never mind all that.

The Word is
the bringer of grace whose face
we long to see.
As we wait, let's be like
Martha's Mary;
let's just sit at his feet,
and listen.

John 1:1–18

School Is In

I used to smirk at those
professional students
haunting the halls of academia
with no discernible plan
to put their study into use
beyond those hallowed halls.
They've got one thing right, though:
the practice of lifelong learning.
As disciples, we step into the waters,
say the Lord's precious name,
and shiver with the promise
that the Holy Spirit
rides the waves of baptism.
But next begins lifelong learning
of the celestial variety, redemption
the only registration required.
Enter the Lord's classroom
and take any seat you like,
or sit at his feet—
a choice long approved.
Swallow the words that fall from
the Teacher's lips,
carry the taste of each revelation
out into a world waiting bird-like
with hungry beaks, then
return to your blood-bought seat
and repeat, and repeat, and repeat.
As for graduation, dear ones,
our diplomas wait in the halls
of heaven.

Acts 19:1–10

Heavenly Haute Couture

We sing songs of sacrifice,
but who, save God, can out-do Hannah?
She humbly offered
what was most precious—
a son to serve her Heavenly Father.
Then, year by year, she clothed her gift
with robes woven of love's devotion.
It's as if Samuel were a gift given again,
and again, and again.
Are we like Samuel?
We come before the Lord naked,
fragile offerings given in response to
God's forgiveness,
then we are called to clothe ourselves
with layers of goodness:
love, kindness and compassion,
gratitude, grace and humility,
patience and the peace of God—
holiness the goal.
But how can we possibly attain it?
How can we begin to gather such threads
to weave a robe of righteousness?
For answers, we must follow
the example set by the Lord
when he was twelve:
we must carry our questions
to the temple,
sit before the rabbi
and lose ourselves
in the teachings
of God.

Colossians 3:12–17, 1 Samuel 2:18–20, 26, Luke 2:41–52

Consequential Choices

We line up for pot-luck,
some skipping soup and salad
in favor of rum cake
and fresh-baked yum!
We sometimes pile our plates with
too many goodies, knowing
full well we'll pay for it later.
Consequential Choices.
The Lord spreads them before us
on the table of each day.
Life and prosperity,
death and adversity;
Love God and walk
in his ways—or don't.
Observe his commands—or not.
His word and will, no secret.
The promise of blessings and curses
sound like a gong within our hearing,
within our own hearts.
Choosing is our one and only
designated part in this drama.
And even in that
slim second of choosing,
Jesus lingers in the
theater of our beings,
coaching us from the wings,
whispering, "Choose Life!
for I am The Way, and The Truth,
and my arms are opened wide—
even in the valley of despair,
disease, depression;
even in the deepest shadows

of pain, of earthquake, heartbreak,
hunger, of not-enough, and
injustice on parade—
these things are temporary. I am not.
Choose Life. Choose me.

Deuteronomy 30:11–20

Mystical Moments

There is something mystical
about moments of *knowing*
that seal the soul.
Sometimes they come
when we listen.
Sometimes, they are
concrete visions from God
that fall as gently as fog,
yet knit themselves,
sturdily as steel cable,
into every cell, every fiber
of one's being,
then, just as suddenly,
lift like mist.
I've had such moments,
and I know, when spoken,
they sound like utter
nonsense, but consider
the surreal moment
of the Magnificat,
or of Gabriel's
personal exchange
with a certain Virgin.
I imagine Mary asking,
"Did that just happen?
Was the Angel Gabriel
really here? Were the words
still ringing in my ear, true?"
In the coming days,
when neighborhood gossips
scandalously question
the timing of
young Mary's pregnancy

once they've done the math
of her betrothal
and marriage date;
later, when her boy, at 12
stays behind in Jerusalem
only to be found
in the temple, teaching
and she and Joseph
wonder why; later still,
when skeptics sneer
at her miracle-working son,
asking what good
can come from Nazareth—
it is precisely at these times,
Mary would call to mind
the visit of Gabriel,
and the mystical minutes
shared with Elizabeth
when the Holy Spirit spoke
to and through them both.
And in that moment
of total recall,
Mary would rest,
and smile,
beatifically.

Luke 1:39–55

A Magi Speaks

I might be mistaken,
but my heart seems
to beat more wildly
with every step we take
toward Bethlehem.
The Holy Family
journeyed here,
beneath the path
of the star.
"Tut-tut!" We urge
our camels over miles
of sand, sun-baked
mud, and rock,
until the fertile foothills
of the Shephelah
are within sight.
There, the star seems
frozen in the sky,
and I sense the end
of our search is near.
My brothers fear
the wrath of Herod,
for I have told them
we cannot return
to his palace as promised.
An angel warned me
in a dream that Herod
means to harm the Child,
and we dare not be
the arrows shot
from Herod's bow.
"Tut-tut!
Come on, my lovely.
The jewel of Bethlehem
sparkles up ahead."

Nazareth Surprise

Faith, hope, and love—
the original 3-point sermon,
a masquerade of simplicity
since love is anything but.
Think: the heart of God,
cracked like an egg,
love spilling everywhere,
red and endless as his passion.
In this age of drive-in weddings
and quick-y divorces,
how can we begin to comprehend?
Forget chocolate and candlelight.
Love is a cup of water,
a warm blanket on a cold night,
a hot cloth on a fevered brow,
a cup of tea steeped in caring.
Love leans into forgiveness,
runs from revenge,
bellies up to the bar of sacrifice.
Love is a life of "You first, ma'am,"
and "Go ahead, sir."
When our moment-by-moment actions
trumpet true love,
the whole world comes running—
well, some do, anyway.
There are always those who say
nothing good can come
from Nazareth.

1 Corinthians 1:1–13, Luke 4:21–30

No Damascus Road

In Corinth, Paul confessed
how uniquely compelled
he was to preach the gospel,
how the risen Jesus
literally stopped him in his tracks.
Well, no Damascus Road for me.
No temporary blindness
hastening the path to surrender.
Mine was a free choice made with
the desperate understanding
that I needed God
to live a life worth living.
And the beauty of his embrace
sent me speeding round
my neighborhood
to show off my new gift
like the true Christmas present
that it was.
"Don't you want redemption, too?"
I asked anyone and everyone
I encountered.
No false righteousness attached.
I was merely a child, giddy with joy
and eager to share it.
Let's all stack the words of the gospel
inside our little red wagons
and joyfully roll them out
into the world.

1 Corinthians 9:16–23

The Glory Story

We've all seen the movie, heard the words,
"Master, now you are dispensing your servant

in peace, according to your word, for my eyes
have seen your salvation." A second prophet

says her piece, then soon enough the screen
fades to black. Film, like life, is a collaborative art,

each person playing a part: Mary, hers; Joseph, his,
silver-haired Simeon and Anna written into the

Christ story, their lines long rehearsed, their
spirit-led lives attentive to the portion of revelation

parceled out to them. How breathlessly they awaited
its unfolding! And what piece of the Glory Story

have *we* been gifted to tend, to share? Do we care
as keenly as God about his story's fulfillment?

It's easy to worry about the whole, harder
to concentrate on our small part, when and

where we're called to put feet on our prayers.
It's this profession that's more than enough to

round out our every day and night, despite how
many moments we're blessed with in the coming
year.

Luke 2:22–40

Human Wisdom

Human wisdom weaves us
a world of trouble
every time. Think Babel,
a towering example of
human wisdom's folly.
We routinely pat ourselves
on the head for the vastness
of our intellectual reservoir.
Babies aren't born of virgins,
only a sorcerer can
turn water into wine,
and no one can raise the dead.
We're all enlightened enough
to understand that, right?
But it might be worth
remembering
that God can speak
through an ass—if he chooses.
He parts the sea one day,
and walks on water the next.
What can our puny power
and whisper-thin wisdom
make of that?
He is God,
and we are not,
and we need Him.

1 Corinthians 1:18–25

Purpose

Obsessed with gravity,
we cling to this small, blue ball.
Yet, to be earthbound
is not what we were made for.
We were made to rise,
to be lifted up by the Lord,
to follow him to
heavenly places.
We are created
to crave the light,
to swallow it whole,
and let its rays
shoot from us,
lighting this dark world
the way stars brighten
the black sky.
What is salvation
if not a call to the light?
But the heights frighten us.
We sometimes prefer
the earthly footpaths
our feet are familiar with,
anything but this
life in the light,
this call to exposure,
to transparency.
Long before the
World Wide Web
the Bible taught us
the importance

of being circumspect,
to expect that,
whatever our deeds,
the Lord will shine
a light on them.
Better to live with him
in the light
in the first place.

John 3:11–21

Seed

How fertile
is your soil?
This question
might seem
rather intimate,
I know. But it goes to
the heart of the matter.
Covenant is the seed
God plants in us,
an investment
in the future
generations,
a call to holiness,
a call to honor
the most High God
for a dividend
beyond measure.
A little faith
is what's required
to release the power
of the promise:
"Walk before me
and be blameless,
and I will establish
my covenant
between me and you,
and your offspring
throughout generations."
That's all it takes to shape
our tomorrows:
a mustard seed of faith

for a mountain
of possibilities.
A pretty good bargain,
don't you think?

Genesis 17:1–7, Romans 4:13–25

Priestly Profession

Whoever gave birth to himself
or chose pain as his partner,
even if glory waited in the wings?
Jesus was chosen as both Son and Priest.
What followed?
Periods of prayer and fasting
lined his life's road like street lights,
there to pierce the gathering gloom.
At twelve, his voice deepened
ahead of adolescence.
No big surprise, perhaps, but
the way the boy's sound settled
into a certain divine authority
was reason to remark.
Time would tell what this meant.
Meanwhile, he'd come to discover
he had a way with wood,
carpentry to be his job,
but priesthood his profession—
since God always has his say.
Fully human, our forerunner
periodically passed through
valleys of tears, crying out loudly
to the father, as we all do when
we're at the end of ourselves,
or in pain, whatever the reason,
and are broken enough
to admit desperation.
Suffering and his obedience through it
was Jesus' path to perfection and to his
becoming our source of salvation.

God, the author of
the true happily-ever-after
made Jesus priest and king forever,
and when we say yes to God—
this is almost too much for me—
he miraculously makes priests of us,
as well.

Hebrews 5:5–10

Reality Check

Death. Wrath. Mercy. Grace.
What a strange and complex
daisy-chain connecting
our past and present—
precisely the reality check
we need to
puncture our egos.
Death came first,
that lonely,
suffocating realm
God's good hand
plucked us from.
Wrath, the anchor
weighing on our souls.
Then came Mercy,
the buoy lifting us
into the realm
of blessing,
of healing,
of belovedness,
of Grace—
A place where we
can breathe,
stand tall,
be a blessing to all
who enter the circle
of our lives,
though no credit
falls to us.
To God be the glory,
for *we* were dead.
Remember?

Ephesians 2:1–10

Under Reconstruction

Under Reconstruction.
Please forgive the mess.
This life of mine, so small, confined
the ceiling low, the windows spare—
Almighty God is living there,
but there's not room
for all his grace, his light
no room to parcel
his love impartially,
his greatness and
his glory cramped,
pressed up against
these thin brown walls.
Something has to give, or go.
It's either God or me.
That's when I feel
the renovation start.
In every room the dynamite is set,
the roof blown off, the ceiling raised,
the windows blasted out, enlarged
the walls of all my prejudices,
my schemes, my plans and dreams
are coming down.
The God of justice is starting fresh.
He's sweeping out this temple,
making me a heart that's clean
with walls of fireproofing glass
through which his light is seen.
He's adding several stories
so that his truth in me can stand,
and if I'm wise enough
to close my eyes,

I can even see his hand
restructuring the framework
of my mind where, one day
I'll find he's made himself
at home.

John 2:13–22

How's My Driving?

I willingly confess:
whatever seed of good
the world sees in me
is compelled by Grace,
by blood poured out from
a love-laced vessel,
generous in purity.
Sturdy in purpose,
his hands, feet, and side
were pierced in payment
for our sins.
We cannot merely watch this
inaugural Passion Play
and do nothing, can we?
Reconciliation is the work
we're meant for,
to be living advertisements
for the good of God,
our need of him,
and the wisdom of aligning
one's abbreviated life
with his everlasting Light.
The key, of course,
to our eventual success
rests in turning to him
at every conceivable juncture
along the way
and asking, "Lord?
How am I doing, so far?"

2 Corinthians 5:14–21

Unfair Trade

"In all your getting, get God,"
I have read. But who gets God?

Who can understand his mind?
I find the question rather esoteric

until I explore more closely. Then
the answer comes, as uncomplicated

as childhood and hopscotch: It takes
one to know one. "Let your minds be

transformed," remember? Spirit to spirit,
true wisdom is translated, the language,

a secret shared between God and us.
His wisdom for our glory, an unfair trade,

on God's part. Yet, wouldn't it be wise for
us to take it? And what is the point of it all?

To burn brightly from within, to shed
God's wisdom and light as we walk through

the world—all salt, all light, all the time.
See? We needn't wrestle with God's will

for our lives. It is simply this:
To know, and to glow.

1 Corinthians 2:1–16, Matthew 5:13–20

No Apology

The still, small voice
comes from within,
part and parcel of
the new covenant,
the one that gives us
entry to an intimacy
with God Almighty.
If we answer the call,
we are all in,
ready and set to go
from darkness to light—
such a sweet invitation!
To serve, and to follow?
Yes! But, wait.
We are also wise
to take into account
the difficult corridors
the Lord's spirit-led steps
sometimes took him to,
and through
—amidst jagged rocks,
past human snakes,
and pausing painfully
in a place of thorns and skulls.
God makes no apology
for the circuitous route
to heaven.
But he promises
we will get there.
He will lead us and love us
on the journey, and our path
will be marked by his glory

and the good he means
to make of us, in us,
and through us,
along the way.

Jeremiah 31:31–34, John 12:20–33

Searching for Amen

Red is the color
of my true love's words,
the hue you and I
are familiar with
as the life-liquid
the Alpha and Omega
spilled to pay for our
triumphal entry
into the gates of heaven.
There we will see
the Tree of Life. When?
"Soon" is his answer.
Soon, David's descendant
will come again.
Blessed news for those
whose robes have been
mysteriously bathed in
the blood that cleanses;
a cause to tremble
for all others.
"Come!" calls the Spirit,
and we say, "Come, Lord."
The gift of this prophecy
is free, but sacred.
Alter one sentence and
suffer the consequences.
Only the beloved
Bright Morning Star,
whose autograph
is authentic,
has the right to pen
the end of his story.

Our meager glory
is to have our names
mentioned within its pages.
That is all the Amen
we will ever need.

Revelation 22:12–21

Tender Mercies

It is easy to wonder
if we are silver, now,
caught in the cauldron
of the refiner's fire.
I can't say. But this I know:
On a day when poetry
can be hard to find,
we cry out to the Lord
for the tender mercies
prophesied by Zechariah.
We count to ten
and breathe in the promise
of dawn breaking over us,
of God's good light
piercing the darkness,
of his steadfast love
seeping into our wounds
like a salve, spreading
the healing we
are desperate for.
Peace, my friends,
awaits us in a certain city
whose holy Architect,
will one day lead us to it.
Until then,
we are blessed to rest
in the arms of
the Prince of Peace,
and for that,
we sing out Hallelujah,
and celebrate his coming,
anew.

Malachi 3:1–4, Luke 1:68–79

ABOUT PARACLETE PRESS

PARACLETE PRESS is the publishing arm of the Cape Cod Benedictine community, the Community of Jesus. Presenting a full expression of Christian belief and practice, we reflect the ecumenical charism of the Community and its dedication to sacred music, the fine arts, and the written word.

SCAN
TO
READ
MORE

www.paracletepress.com

IRON PEN

O that my words were written down!
O that they were inscribed in a book!
O that with an iron pen and with lead
they were engraved on a rock forever!
—JOB 19:23–24

Outcast and utterly alone, Job pours out his anguish to his Maker. From the depths of his pain, he reveals a trust in God's goodness that is stronger than his despair, giving humanity some of the most beautiful and poetic verses of all time. Paraclete's Iron Pen imprint is inspired by this spirit of unvarnished honesty and tenacious hope.

You may also be interested in

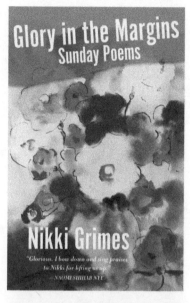

www.paracletepress.com

Which
Seeds
Will
Grow?

poems

Andrew J. Calis

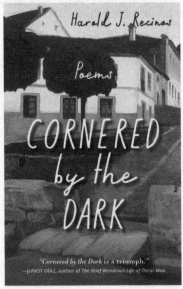

Harold J. Recinos

Poems

CORNERED
by the
DARK

"Cornered by the Dark is a triumph."
—JUNOT DÍAZ, author of The Brief Wondrous Life of Oscar Wao